ELTHAM PALACE

BY MICHAEL TURNER, PhD

ENGLISH HERITAGE, LONDON

CONTENT

D0508033

GREAT HALL

SOUTH TIMBER BRIDGE

ENTRANCE TO HOUSE
and TOILETS

SQUASH COURT

SUNKEN ROSE GARDEN

TICKET OFFICE,
SHOP and TEA ROOM

NORTH STONE BRIDGE

CHAUFFEUR'S COTTAGE

ILLUSTRATION BY PETER DUNN

The remains of Eltham Palace from the north-east, engraved by Samuel and Nathaniel Buck in 1735

INTRODUCTION

Eltham Palace is one of the few important medieval royal palaces in England to survive with substantial remains intact. Initially a moated manor house, it was acquired by the future Edward II in 1305 who subsequently passed it on to his queen, Isabella. Under Edward IV significant changes were made, most notably the addition of the Great Hall in the 1470s which is still visible today. Eltham Palace was eclipsed by Greenwich Palace in the sixteenth century and declined rapidly: for 200 years after the Civil War it was a farm.

In the 1930s an important private house, boasting an ultra-modern design and use of technology, was built adjoining the Great Hall. The moving force behind this unexpected development was a wealthy couple, Stephen and Virginia Courtauld, who in 1933 sought a semi-rural property within easy reach of central London. Eltham met their requirements and the architects Seely and Paget were commissioned to restore the Great Hall and design a new adjoining home. Leading designers and craftsmen were employed to create a range of lavish interiors and outstanding gardens, providing the setting for Stephen and Virginia's extensive collection of art and furniture, and ample space for entertaining.

The Courtaulds left Eltham in 1944 and the site was occupied by Army educational units until 1992. English Heritage assumed management of the palace in 1995, and in 1999 completed a major programme of repairs to and restoration of the 1930s interiors and gardens.

This souvenir guidebook contains a description of the stunning 1930s interiors, the medieval remains and the gardens, followed by an account of the development and context of this extraordinary site.

The curved colonnade and staircase pavilions of the new house by Seely and Paget

Stephen and Virginia Courtauld

Stephen Courtauld was born in 1883, the youngest of six children. By 1912 the Courtauld family owned a highly successful business empire based on the manufacture of rayon (artificial or 'art' silk). Although Stephen did not join the firm his inherited shares generated a substantial fortune, which he used to pursue a wide variety of cultural and philanthropic interests.

At the onset of the First World War Stephen joined the Artists' Rifles and in 1918 he was awarded the Military Cross and rose to the rank of Major. After the war he resumed one of his greatest passions – mountaineering in the Alps. In 1919 he and his climbing companion E G Oliver completed the pioneer ascent of the Innominata face of Mont Blanc.

In the same year Stephen met Virginia Peirano at Courmayeur in the Alps. 'Ginie' was the daughter of an Italian father and Hungarian mother, and was a divorced marchesa (marchioness) by her former marriage to an Italian aristocrat. Stephen and Ginie were married in August 1923. In many ways they were an unlikely couple. Ginie had a lively Italian temperament: vivacious, full of laughter, impulsive and chic – she had a snake tattooed just above her right ankle. Stephen, on the other hand, tended to be cautious and reserved; he thought much, but said little. As a friend and former colleague wrote: 'He was very much our Rock of Gibraltar – always the same, good days and bad, completely unflappable. He never used two words where one would do.'

The Courtaulds had no children, but from 1926 they looked after two nephews of Ginie's – Peter and Paul Peirano, born in 1916 and 1918 respectively. Both Stephen and Ginie were very fond of the young, and it is characteristic that in many of their activities they encouraged individuals at the start of their career.

The couple were also enthusiastic supporters of the arts scene. Stephen was a trustee of Covent Garden Opera House and made a large donation towards the construction of the Courtauld Galleries in the Fitzwilliam Museum, Cambridge. In 1926 he built the London Ice Club – the first post-war ice-skating rink in the country.

Design and Plan of the House

The Courtaulds met Seely and Paget in 1933. This was the young architects' first important commission. Their aim at Eltham was to design a modern home on the site of the nineteenth-century buildings while retaining as much as possible of the remains of the royal palace. Their design was fairly restrained: the exterior was of brick and Clipsham stone, while modern building materials such as reinforced concrete were concealed from view. It was inspired by Wren's Hampton Court Palace on the mistaken assumption that Wren was 'restoring', rather than seeking to rebuild, the Tudor palace.

The most outstanding feature of the new house, apart from its setting, is the glamorous treatment and quality of its interiors. Eclecticism is a keyword of 1930s internal decoration, and at Eltham the styles range from 'historical' (the Drawing Room) to the new aesthetic of the 1930s (the Dining Room). Such variety reflects the tastes of the Courtaulds and their artistic advisers: the painters Winifred Knights and her husband Tom Monnington, the Swedish interior designer Rolf Engströmer and the Italian decorator Peter Malacrida. Typical details include walls lined with native and exotic woods, and the use of pale paint colours, which was a move away from the strong colours favoured by the Edwardians.

The Courtauld interiors are described in detail in the following tour. For more information about the Courtaulds and their life at Eltham, turn to pages 34–40.

L Campbell Taylor's portrait of the Courtaulds with their lemur Mah-Jongg in the Music Room of 47 Grosvenor Square, 1934. At Eltham, it hung on the principal landing at the top of the west stairs

The Entrance Hall with the recreated Engströmer furniture and Dorn carpet. Engströmer designed similar furniture for Stockholm University in 1935

OPPOSITE *'Hospitality' by H Carlton Attwood*

THE COURTAULD HOUSE

Exterior

Your tour of Eltham Palace begins with the house built by the Courtaulds in the 1930s. Standing outside the main entrance, you can appreciate some of the design features of the building. The curved entrance colonnade is flanked by two tall, copper-clad pavilions with models of chessmen on the roof ridges. The green-painted metal casement windows are typical of the 1930s. The infilled arches of the colonnade are copied from Wren's Hampton Court and the Library at Trinity College, Cambridge (attended by Seely and Paget). The junction between the 1930s building and the medieval Great Hall to your right is marked by a projecting spiral staircase with a stone cap. The 1930s exterior is enlivened by a number of sculptures. Over the arch to the main entrance is a work by H Carlton Attwood representing Hospitality, inviting you to enter.

Entrance Hall

To the left and right are the gentlemen's and ladies' cloakrooms – a location more typical of an institution than a private house, but reflecting the importance of entertaining at Eltham.

Glazed double doors lead into the Entrance Hall, which is triangular in plan with rounded corners. Light floods through the concrete glass domed roof, which is 23 feet (7m) in diameter – a feature specifically requested by Stephen Courtauld. The internal design of this space was by the Swedish designer Rolf Engströmer.

The hall is completely lined with Australian blackbean veneer, and incorporates a marquetry panel by the Swedish artist Jerk Werkmäster on either side of the entrance doors. The panel comprises a Roman soldier and a Viking against background scenes from Italy and Scandinavia. Some of the Courtaulds' favourite buildings are represented, including palaces in Florence and Venice, and various buildings in

Scenes from Lewis Carroll's Alice *books by Eric Grate. The setting of the story within a dream appealed to Grate who was a prominent figure in Swedish Surrealist art (based on the visual representation of dreams)*

Part of the marquetry panelling depicting Stockholm Town Hall

Stockholm such as the 1920s Town Hall. Above the entrance are two plaques supplied by another Swede, Eric Grate. They depict scenes from Lewis Carroll's *Alice* books.

A circular rug by the well-established and influential textile and carpet designer Marion Dorn, measuring 19 feet (5.8m) in diameter, was commissioned for the centre of the hall. Its shades of reddish brown, pinkish beige and fawn complemented the marquetry designs on the walls. The rug is now at the Victoria and Albert Museum and the present rug is a replica. The Entrance Hall curtains were doubtless also designed by Dorn, who favoured horizontal bands. The blackbean and walnut furniture, with fashionable cream loose covers edged with piping, was designed by Engströmer specifically for this room; the replicas you see today are based on the original designs.

At the far side of the Entrance Hall, to the left of the french windows, is a booth (not open to visitors) containing a coin-operated telephone for the use of guests – telephone calls were expensive in the 1930s. To the right of the

ROLF ENGSTRÖMER
(1892–1970)

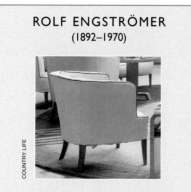

One of the original Engströmer tub chairs photographed by Country Life *in 1936*

Engströmer trained as an architect but quickly developed a reputation for furniture design. By 1933 he had established his own architectural firm and was head of a Swedish furnishing and decoration company, Jefta. His refined design for Eltham was described in 1937 in *Country Life* as 'probably the first example in this country of modern Swedish decoration originated by Ostberg at the Stockholm Town Hall' (the latter had been visited by Stephen and Ginie in 1928 and was a place of pilgrimage for young English architects at the time). The Swedish style became popular in the 1950s and is still highly influential – via Ikea – today.

windows is the Flower Room (not open), which housed a sink and over eighty vases in which to prepare and arrange cut flowers from the gardens. It also contains a bamboo ladder which allowed Mah-Jongg (Jongy) – the Courtaulds' pet ring-tailed lemur – to descend from his first-floor quarters.

Drawing Room

The entrance to the Drawing Room is to the right of the Flower Room. A hint of the original sumptuous appearance of this room is provided by the reproduction soft furnishings: the silk damask curtains and the sofas covered in blue velvet. The room was designed by Peter Malacrida (see page 15) for the firm White Allom and incorporates a number of items salvaged from the Music Room of the Courtaulds' former home at 47 Grosvenor Square. These include the cupboard doors on either side of the entrance doors and the dark green iron screens on the french windows next to the chimneybreast. The marble fireplace is Italian in inspiration and was probably designed by Malacrida, while the decoration on the plaster false beams imitates Hungarian folk art (the combination referring to Ginie's Italo-Hungarian parentage). The hollow beams accommodated concealed lighting directed on to the paintings – a sophisticated device recently imported from Paris. The walls and ceilings were painted cream, with a thin honey-coloured glazing on top.

The plaster panels in the window reveals were designed by Gilbert Ledward in 1935. They represent the four quarters of the world as illustrated by various civilisations throughout history and refer to the ideas of the German philosopher Oswald Spengler. Spengler's thesis, which he expounded in *The Decline of the West* (first published in English in 1926), was based on the premise that all civilisations would eventually decline through decadence and mankind would once more be forced to live off the land as an 'eternal peasant'. From left to right, the panels represent: Northern (Caesarism contrasted with the Eternal Peasant), Southern (Southern World and Primitive Life), Eastern (Mystic East and Ancient World), Western (Classical World contrasted with Modern

One of the plaster ceiling beams painted to look like timber. The decoration was inspired by Hungarian folk art

World). Above each relief are alternate coats of arms of the Courtaulds and the Peiranos (the latter representing a lion grasping a pear tree).

The floor was laid with antique 'Turkish' rugs. The room was designed to display the Courtaulds' collection of Italian walnut furniture and pictures, such as the large Venetian School *Contest of Apollo and Marsayas* and Cosimo Rosselli's *Madonna*, above and to the left of the chimneypiece. The room also housed two Veroneses, *Astronomer* and *Patriarch* (on loan from the National Gallery of Zimbabwe), and the most outstanding single painting in the collection, *Christ in Limbo* by Andrea Mantegna (now in the USA). Where necessary, alternative paintings have now been hung to give an impression of the original effect.

The cupboards and niches housed almost thirty pieces of Italian porcelain – mostly

sixteenth-century Majolica whose vibrant colours would have acted as a foil to the cream-coloured walls.

GILBERT LEDWARD
(1888–1960)

Ledward won a scholarship to the British School in Rome in 1913 and later became Professor of Sculpture at the Royal College of Art. His most prominent London work is probably the Guards' Memorial at Horseguards Parade (like Stephen Courtauld he joined the Artists' Rifles in the First World War.) Spengler's theory of decline appealed to Ledward in relation to modern art, particularly the move away from realism towards abstraction. We must assume Stephen Courtauld was also sympathetic to these views.

ABOVE *Ledward's 'Modern World' shows modern man standing on top of an Ionic column surveying factories and aeroplanes. It is contrasted with 'Classical World' showing Icarus attempting to fly. Together they suggest modern achievement and its debt to classical civilisation*

The Drawing Room photographed in 1936

Great Hall Corridor

On leaving the Drawing Room, the door immediately to your left leads into the corridor to the Great Hall. Above this door is a loudspeaker which was connected to a mahogany record cabinet in the corridor from which music could be broadcast throughout the ground floor. Next to it was a wireless set with seven pairs of speakers in a cabinet designed to look like an old Italian walnut coffer. On the left-hand side of the corridor are two doors leading first to the Boudoir and then the Library.

Boudoir

Ginie Courtauld's panelled Boudoir was designed by Malacrida. The fashion for ceilings to be painted a lighter tint of the wall colour can be seen here, as in many of the main rooms. The ribbed, coved and mirrored ceiling with its concealed lighting is Art Deco-inspired. The sofa is an early example of built-in furniture. It has Italian quilted cushions with a raised design (quilting was a popular hobby in the 1930s). The shelves once held assorted French novels. The Boudoir contained a McMichael wireless set in a walnut case, with an art silk cover. McMichael radios were hand-made and considered to be the best available. Above the sofa is a large painting after Jan Wyck, *Frost Fair on the Thames in 1684* (a copy of the original). To the right of the fireplace is a leather-covered jib (hidden) door which communicated with the Library (now not in use).

The Secretary's office was entered via the arch to the right of the sofa. In 1939 this room was described as the Map Room on account of the maps which were pasted to the walls to help her arrange the Courtaulds' overseas tours. The office contained three telephones – part of the internal and external telephone systems. It is hoped to restore this room at a later date.

RIGHT Detail of Eltham Palace on the leather map. The leather has faded considerably, and the original effect would have been similar to 1930s posters, with their bold blocks of colour

The sofa. Country Life commented in 1932: 'One of the most sensible and convenient of recent pieces of furniture is the couch that combines shelves for the current library books and cross-word dictionaries, with place to put down a cup of tea or a glass'

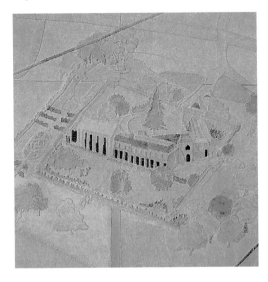

Leather Map

In the later seventeenth and early eighteenth centuries grand property-owners displayed maps and bird's-eye views of their estates. The leather map above the fireplace, depicting Eltham Palace and its surroundings, is a revival of this tradition. It combines a map with topographical views and was created, according to *Country Life*, by Mrs Classen Smith.

Eltham is at the centre of the map. In the bottom left-hand corner is the Woolwich coat of arms and the borough motto, 'Clamant querela nostra Regis tela in Woolwich' ('In Woolwich, our weapons ring out with the king's complaint') – a reference to Woolwich Arsenal. The bottom right-hand corner depicts Napoleon III and his consort Eugénie, who were exiled to nearby Chislehurst in 1871. The map stretches as far as the Thames to the north, and illustrates, amongst other places, the former Royal Naval College and Observatory with the meridian passing through it, the Royal Arsenal at Woolwich, Lewisham clock tower and the Crystal Palace (which burned down in 1936).

LEFT *The Library. The original Tabriz medallion carpet (not shown) was returned to this room in 2003*

BELOW *Stephen Courtauld's telephone. Stephen did not like the telephone and this one could make internal calls only*

Library

The Library, again by Malacrida, is lined with what *Country Life* described as 'Indian Mahogany'. It accommodated Stephen Courtauld's collection of watercolours and other topographical works by artists such as J R Cozens, Paul Sandby, Thomas Girtin and John Sell Cotman. They included fourteen Turners (now in the Courtauld Institute; those on display are copies). They were protected by ingenious vertically sliding shutters designed by Stephen, probably inspired by a similar arrangement in Sir John Soane's house in Lincoln's Inn Fields. On the outside of the shutters was a collection of woodcuts, etchings and engravings, including works by Albrecht Dürer and Turner. Among the books were standard reference works such as the *Dictionary of National Biography* and *Encyclopaedia Britannica*, as well as those representing more specialist interests such as

mountaineering, exploration, Greek and Roman coins, history and art. Architectural and topographical books included works on the medieval palace of Eltham. The Library also housed Stephen's extensive collection of English lustre-ware porcelain and his coin collection.

The walnut desk (a replica) sits in front of a recess housing a pull-down roller map. Opposite is a fireplace, with a niche above containing a bronze statuette, *The Sentry*. This sculpture was purchased from Charles Sargeant Jagger in 1924 as a reduced copy of his war memorial in Manchester. Like Stephen, Jagger had joined the Artists' Rifles during the First World War and was awarded the Military Cross in 1918. The profound significance of the subject for Stephen Courtauld is suggested by its prominent position in the room. The present statuette is a cast of the original.

Stephen Courtauld's bookplate, depicting Apollo, was designed and engraved in 1925 by Stephen Gooden. The family has generously returned many of the original books to the house

LEFT *Replica of* The Sentry *by Charles Sargeant Jagger, 1924*

Great Hall

The end of the corridor leading to the Great Hall is lined by a 1920s or 1930s copy of a twelve-panelled Chinese Coromandel screen (so called because they were exported to Europe in large quantities via the Coromandel Coast of south-east India). Beyond the screen you enter the Great Hall. Although this was incorporated into the 1930s house, the hall was originally part of the great medieval palace, and was built for Edward IV in the 1470s as a dining hall for the court.

Like many other medieval great halls, it is composed of a high end, with a raised platform or dais where the king or lord would have dined, and a low, or service, end (where you are now standing). At the service end was a 'screens passage' which shielded the main hall from draughts from the external doors. The two blocked doors in the passage led to the medieval buttery and pantry; the kitchen was in a courtyard beyond the door at the far end of the passage.

The hall measures 101ft by 36ft (30.8m by 10.9m) and 55ft (16.8m) tall to the apex of the roof. It is comparable in size with the Great Hall at Hampton Court built in the 1520s. The magnificent oak roof is an elaborate false hammerbeam construction (described as 'false' because the posts are morticed into the ends of the hammerbeams rather than resting on the beams). It is decorated with fine tracery and there is evidence that it was once partly gilded. Near the dais end of the hall was a hearth, doubtless with a louvre in the roof above for smoke to escape. The high windows allowed light to flood in and were decorated with stained glass. The extensive wall space below was

NATIONAL MONUMENTS RECORD

probably lined with tapestries when the court was in residence. At the dais end two double-height oriel (bay) windows give further light and emphasis to the most important part of the hall. Some of the damaged stone bosses (ornaments) at the centre of the vaulting in each bay were replaced in timber by Seely and Paget. Two doors in the end bays originally led to the king's and queen's apartments beyond the hall; they now lead to the orangery and squash court added by the Courtaulds.

The Courtaulds intended the Great Hall to be used as a music room. They carried out repairs to the medieval fabric, introduced modern comforts such as central-heating pipes under the floor, and made a series of interventions that might be described as 'antiquarian revival'. These latter represent Stephen Courtauld's (and his architects') view of what a medieval Great Hall should be like. They may also have been influenced by the contemporary film industry's view of Tudor England: in 1933, the year the Courtaulds found Eltham, Charles Laughton starred in *The Private Life of Henry VIII*. Examples of this work include the Minstrels' Gallery, which is pure invention and not based on evidence. The timber screen at the dais end was a speculative addition by Seely and Paget based on the fifteenth-century rood screen in Attleborough Church, Norfolk. Above the canopy are coloured shields of various monarchs associated with the hall, while on the tracery beneath are the initials of the individuals mainly responsible for the restoration work: JWH (John Hopkins,

RIGHT When the Great Hall at Eltham was built, it was the largest of its kind with the exception of Westminster Hall, shown here, built in the 1090s

Edward IV's badges in stained glass by Kruger Gray

COZENS COLLECTION

Caesar - the Courtaulds' Great Dane – sitting on an Italian 'Doge's' chair in the Great Hall in 1940

Clerk of Works), SLC and VC (Stephen and Ginie), CP (Charles Peers – see page 34), JS (John Seely), PEP (Paul Paget) and WKM (Winifred Knights Monnington).

Stained glass was added in 1936 by George Kruger Gray – one of the foremost designers of coins, medals and stained glass. The roundels depict the badges of Edward IV: the sun in splendour, the Yorkist white rose, the 'rose en soleil' and the falcon and fetterlock. Stained glass in the bay windows at the dais end depicts some of the great owners of the palace: Bishops Odo and Bek, Edward I, Edward III, Richard II and Henry VIII in the south (left-hand) bay, and Edward IV and his queen Elizabeth in the north. On the walls are modern copies of the ten metal sconces with coronet surmounts which were probably designed by Seely; behind these hung 'art' silk (rayon) hangings made by Courtaulds and given by Stephen's brother Sam. The current hangings date from the 1980s.

A wooden roof boss depicting Mah-Jongg in the north bay

The Great Hall in the late 1930s

The restoration work was commemorated by a Latin inscription in the southern bay window; this can be translated as: 'This hall, which the great King Edward built in former days, having fallen into increasing ruin, has now been restored through the care of Virginia and Stephen'. Below, in English, is an inscription summarising the history of the site as it was then understood, which was added at the suggestion of Queen Mary: 'This hall was built by Edward IV in the year 1479, the Bridge over the Moat by Richard II in 1396, & the Moat Walls by Anthony Bek, Bishop of Durham about the year 1300.'

The Courtaulds filled their 1930s version of a medieval hall with antique furniture – mostly seventeenth-century English and European – which remains in the hall today. Much of this was purchased specifically for the Great Hall, including the large yew table in the centre of the hall, and the sixteenth-century 21ft- (6.4m-) long oak refectory table. Although 1930s and '40s photographs show the room in use as a sitting room, the Great Hall really came into its own as a reception room for large parties.

West Stairs

Return along the corridor and into the Entrance Hall. The blackbean veneered sweeping stairs and balustrades on either side of the main entrance were the work of Engströmer, but Seely designed the large circular portholes. Take the stairs to the left of the entrance as you face it. The large expanse of wall on the staircase is partially covered by Andrea Piazza's oil painting *The King of Poland Being Received by the Doge of Venice*, which is on loan from the National Gallery of Zimbabwe. Stephen Courtauld admitted the painting was bought 'to fill an unsightly blank piece of staircase wall … it is an amusing rather grey painting of some historical interest but not very much artistic merit.'

The statuary bust of Ginie on the Principal Landing was carved by F Lovatelli in 1923

HULTON GETTY

Principal Landing and Minstrels' Gallery

Prominently hung on the pale blue landing is a copy of L Campbell Taylor's stunning 1934 portrait of the Courtaulds with their lemur (see page 3). Take the corridor to your right. This leads to the Minstrels' Gallery, created by the Courtaulds to provide a superb view of the Great Hall. Music recitals were sometimes given here. On the floor and balcony you can see scorch marks caused by an incendiary bomb which fell during the Battle of Britain in September 1940.

Stephen Courtauld's Suite

Returning along the corridor, the first two doors on the right led to the rooms of Ginie's nephews Peter and Paul Peirano (not open to visitors). Beyond is Stephen's suite, which was designed by Seely. This consists of an aspen-lined bedroom, a walk-in wardrobe and a blue-and green-tiled bathroom. On the side walls of the bedroom is a block-printed wallpaper depicting Kew Gardens made by Sandersons;

Stephen Courtauld's bedroom and the view into his tile-lined bathroom

A detail of the Rust's vitreous mosaic tiling which imparts a Mediterranean air to Stephen's bathroom

the coved ceiling represents the sky linking the two landscapes.

Among the pictures which originally hung in the bedroom were images of people Stephen admired: Beethoven, whose late string quartets were particular favourites; Julius Caesar, revered for his skill as an historian; and Ginie, a photograph of whose statuary bust by Lovatelli stood on the shelf above the corner fire.

Stephen's bedroom photographed in 1936. The Kew Gardens wallpaper was rarely produced as the process of hand-printing so many blocks was very costly

RIGHT *Virginia Courtauld's bedroom*

BELOW *A primitive temple is represented on the entrance door. Many details on the door correspond to the appearance of the bedroom: the columns of the temple are echoed in the sycamore pilasters; the flaming torches are suggested by the light brackets around the room, whose crystal figures diffused the light*

ABOVE *The curved door to the bathroom is inlaid with marquetry showing Ginie's initials and a floating boat*

RIGHT *Virginia Courtauld's bathroom*

Virginia Courtauld's Bedroom

Ginie's suite is much more flamboyant in its design than Stephen's – reflecting both her character and that of Malacrida, the designer. The bedroom is approached via a circular lobby, with three niches for flowers, and a curved sliding door.

With its curved walls lined with maple flexwood, Ginie's bedroom has the appearance of a primitive temple. A classical shrine once sat within the alcove above the bed. The room contains classical allusions to three of the four elements: copies of two paintings by Jan Breughel represent *Air with Daphne and her Suitor Apollo*, and *Water with Neptune and his Wife Amphitrite*, while fire is alluded to, appropriately enough on either side of the electric fire, in the incised depictions of a salamander and a phoenix – mythical creatures which rose out of the flames. Rectangular recesses at either end of the bedroom contained a dressing table and cupboards. The main light source and the central heating are concealed within the circular ceiling.

Virginia Courtauld's Bathroom

The exotic ensuite bathroom was also designed by Malacrida. It is the most opulent in the house, and accords with *Vogue*'s comment in 1935: 'Bathrooms nowadays look more expensive than any rooms in the house'. It has a vaulted ceiling and walls lined with onyx and embellished with black slate disks on to which were set glass spheres. The bath has gold-plated taps and a lion's-mask spout. It sits within a gold mosaic niche containing a statue of the goddess Psyche (the lover of Cupid). This combination of classical statuary and modern design followed the latest Parisian vogue. The original statue was bought in Naples in 1924 by Stephen Courtauld but was later sold; however, an identical one, bought at about the same time by Stephen's sister Catherine, was given in 1999 by a member of the family. The bathroom is filled with the fragrance of gardenia – Ginie's habitual scent.

COUNTRY LIFE

PETER MALACRIDA
(c.1889–c.1980)

The gold-plated basin taps in Ginie's bathroom

Peter Malacrida (the Marchese Malacrida) had something of the reputation of an Italian playboy in the 1920s and '30s. Just after the First World War he became a newspaper correspondent and in 1922 married Nadja, who wrote plays under the pen name 'Lewis Hope'. The Malacridas were personal friends of the Courtauld family; they were great entertainers and popular with the 'young West End set', according to the author Cecil Roberts. Malacrida took to interior design, specialising in a Florentine renaissance style. In the late 1920s and early '30s he and his wife were near neighbours of Stephen and Ginie in Grosvenor Square, and he carried out work both for them and for Sam Courtauld. His designs were regarded as sensational.

During the Depression Malacrida joined the firm White Allom where his social contacts with clients were extremely useful. However, in 1940 he returned to Italy to fight in the war; he subsequently retired to southern Ireland.

Mah-Jongg's Quarters

Return to the principal landing, turn right past the remains of the fifteenth-century timber windows of the palace and follow the corridor to the quarters of 'Jongy', the Courtaulds' ring-tailed lemur. Jongy was bought at Harrods in 1923. He was a much-loved pet who remained with them for fifteen years, accompanying them on their travels and changes of residence. Jongy was infamous for biting people to whom he took a dislike. On the morning of the departure of the 1930–31 British Arctic expedition, sponsored by Stephen, the Courtaulds gave a farewell lunch on board their yacht, the *Virginia*; the expedition suffered a severe setback when Jongy bit the hand of Percy Lemon, the expedition's wireless operator, severing an artery. Lemon turned out to be allergic to the iodine which was provided, and it took him three months to recover.

Jongy's sleeping quarters were centrally heated. The walls were originally decorated with bamboo forest scenes by Miss G E Whinfield, and a bamboo ladder enabled him to descend to the ground-floor Flower Room.

LEFT *Mah-Jongg posing for* Country Life *in his sleeping quarters in 1936. The walls were redecorated in imitation of the lost original in 2001 by Clare Bailey of Peter Farlow*

BELOW *Jongy died at Eltham in 1938 and the Courtaulds commissioned a memorial from Ledward's firm, Memorials and Statues. This comprised a banded obelisk in imitation of the lemur's tail and a lead relief of Jongy. It was initially erected in the grounds at Eltham but is now at La Rochelle, the Courtaulds' last home in Zimbabwe*

MICHAEL TURNER

RIGHT *The Japanese Room
– a walnut-lined guest
bedroom with built-in
furniture by Seely and
Paget. Among the books
provided for guests were
E M Forster's* Howards
End *(1910) and Vera
Brittain's* Testament of
Youth *(1933)*

*The unrestored Venetian
Bedroom with a late
seventeenth-century Italian
'tabernacle' (left) and false
book spines (right)*

The windows opposite give a good view of
the rock garden beyond the moat, while further
along the corridor the window on the left
overlooks the glazed dome of the Entrance Hall
and the contrasting timber gables from the
palace.

Venetian Suite

The Venetian suite was one of two guest double
bedrooms. It was designed to accommodate
some fragments of 1780s Venetian panelling
which were initially installed in Ginie
Courtauld's bedroom in Grosvenor Square.
Malacrida added a screen of three arches on the
window wall, and arabesque designs painted on
to mirrors. The entrance and cupboard doors
are embellished with false book spines.

The bathroom was probably designed by
Seely. It is lined with yellow Vitrolite – rolled
glass panels manufactured by Pilkington from
1932. Vitrolite was considered at the time to be
the ultimate hygienic easy-clean surface. It was
commonly produced in white but yellow was
much rarer and a sign of luxury. This suite was
occupied by Ginie's mother when she visited
England and the bathroom is the only one in
the house to contain a bidet – considered the
height of European bathroom chic.

COUNTRY LIFE

Guest Bedroom Suites

Leading off the lobby is an adjoining dressing
room which formed part of the Venetian suite.
Known as the Pear Room on account of its
pearwood bed, it could function as a separate
guest bedroom if required. The single guest
bedrooms such as this were economical in their
use of space but provided sufficient
accommodation for a comfortable stay. They
were designed by Seely, with built-in laminated
wood furniture with curved ends and horizontal
lines reminiscent of cabins in an ocean liner.
The bar handles are typical of those favoured
by Modern Movement architects in the early
1930s. The rooms were heated by an electric
fire and equipped with an internal telephone
and electric clock. The bathrooms have
distinctive chrome fittings and often a sunken
bath with a shelf alongside. All ten of the
ensuite bathrooms at Eltham could be supplied
with sufficient hot water for baths at the same
time – a demanding specification.

Leave the Pear Room and turn right into the
corridor. The remaining rooms on this floor are
not open to the public. They include two
further guest bedrooms and the Secretary's
room, occupied by Miss Violet Torckler (known
as 'Torckie'). One of the rooms is marked
'Batmen' – a relic, along with the room
numbers, of the Army's occupation of Eltham.
Beyond the double doors were bedrooms for the
ten resident servants: Ginie's maid and three
housemaids, Miss Emma Truckle the cook, two
kitchen maids, a butler and two footmen. The
East Staircase, to the left, leads back down to
the Entrance Hall. At the bottom, immediately
to the left, are double doors leading into the
service wing. The main doors beyond lead into
the Dining Room.

Dining Room

The Dining Room, designed by Malacrida, exemplifies the sophisticated 'Moderne' style which tended to favour geometrical or stylised shapes rather than the organic forms of the earlier Art Nouveau. Malacrida may have been influenced by schemes such as the dining room at the Galeries Lafayette shown at the seminal Paris *Exposition des Arts Décoratifs* of 1925, from which the term 'Art Deco' was later coined. The design relies on contrasting tones and textures for effect. The walls are lined with bird's-eye maple flexwood, as are the ceiling cove and picture frames. In dramatic contrast the recessed central portion of the ceiling is entirely covered in aluminium leaf on a blue background, with built-in concealed lighting to make the metal shimmer at night; around the perimeter are aluminium-covered rose-shaped ornaments (paterae). A comparable ceiling of the same period can be found in the Ballroom of the Park Lane Hotel, Piccadilly. The floor has a black marble perimeter surrounding a reproduction buff carpet with a brown and black border. The fireplace consists of polished, ribbed aluminium panels surrounding the original electric fire which still retains its imitation logs illuminated by electric bulbs. It has a black Belgian marble

The Dining Room chimneypiece, with a replica of Bonneville Savoy *by J M W Turner (Yale Center for British Art, Paul Mellon Collection)*

surround inlaid with a Greek key pattern. This classical motif, which is repeated on the ebonised doors and side tables, was often used in the 1930s. Two ancient Greek amphorae (jars) stood on the sideboard, and the whole effect suggests the atrium of a Roman house. The built-in cabinets have glass shelves and

A Christmas dinner party, early 1940s. The paintings were removed for the duration of the war. Left to Right: Ginie, August Courtauld (RNVR), Edward Keeling (formerly British Consul-General at Tangier), Violet Torckler, Iliffe Cozens (RAF), Mollie Courtauld, Stephen (Civil Defence), Peter Peirano, Sir George Binney (Lt Commander, RNVR), Major George Courtauld (Stephen's cousin and then Director of Personnel in the Special Operations Executive) and his wife Claudine

ABOVE *A cupboard door in the Dining Room with applied lacquer animals and birds by the little-known artist Narini*

The Dining Room. Dinner was at 8pm with a menu written in French; courses were accompanied by vintage nineteenth- and early twentieth-century wines

mirror backs – typical Art Deco features; they contained a selection of ancient Persian and Chinese pottery and porcelain. (The ceramics currently on display give a sense of the colours and designs of the originals.) The striking doors feature animals and birds drawn from life at London Zoo, and applied as ivory-coloured raised decoration. The significance of the choice of subjects is not known.

The furniture was rediscovered in 2000. It was reproduced, including the dining chairs with pink leather upholstery (rose pink was considered at the time to be 'an ideal colour for setting off ladies' dresses to the best advantage'). The pictures – all landscapes – evidently formed part of the original plan for the room since the frames are ensuite with the room. Reading clockwise from just to the left of the entrance doors, they were: *The Limekiln* by John Crome, *Near Keswick* by Peter de Wint, *Lake Nemi* by Richard Wilson, *The River Brent* and *Bonneville, Savoy*, both by J M W Turner, and *The Falls at Inverary* by Patrick Naysmith. One of the Turners has been reproduced with the help of the National Gallery, London. The original Crome was purchased with the assistance of the National Art Collections Fund.

In addition to the electric fire, the room was heated by heating coils embedded in the central ceiling panel. On the end wall are a circular barometer and electric clock, while on the wall opposite the fireplace is a loudspeaker which was connected to the record cabinet.

Service Wing

The door to the left of the loudspeaker leads into a servery. It is lined with white Vitrolite with a green band, and on the left is a silver safe. This contained a 1935 silver service commissioned for the house, and over sixty pieces of Courtauld-made silver dating from 1716–78 (the Courtaulds were originally gold- and silversmiths). The servery contains the food

BRITISH ARCHITECTURAL LIBRARY, RIBA, LONDON

lift connecting to the first floor. At the far end is a lobby leading to the Kitchen (now the tea room). The kitchen fittings are now gone but they included some of the first stainless steel sinks and two Jackson's electric cookers. English Heritage has attempted to restore some of the room's original character. Beyond the Kitchen is the shop, formerly the servants' hall.

For safety reasons the basement is closed to visitors. It contains the motor for the vacuum cleaner, Stephen Courtauld's photographic dark room, a games room and billiards room. There are also cellars surviving from the nineteenth-century house (see page 33); these in turn were formed out of the palace remains. The basement has a reinforced concrete ceiling and the cellars were used as air-raid shelters throughout the war.

ABOVE *The Kitchen in 1936 showing the two electric cookers and a fine set of green and white storage jars. One of the original fitted cupboards survived the Army alterations and has been restored*

ABOVE LEFT *Representation of an iguana from the Galapagos Islands on the cupboard doors in the Dining Room*

Part of a mural to *St Cecilia (patron saint of music) by Mary Adshead, formerly in the Music Room at 47 Grosvenor Square and relocated to the Billard Room in the basement. The lemur represents Jongy*

Stephen and Ginie conceived ambitious plans for their new gardens at Eltham. Today they are a rare and very fine example of 1930s garden design that is open to the public. The fact that they incorporate elements of the medieval palace adds a further intriguing dimension. The tour that follows this introduction includes all the main garden features.

Design of the Courtauld Gardens

Before the creation of the gardens could begin, some of the existing retaining walls were rebuilt and the moat was partially re-excavated and flooded. An initial design for the gardens was produced by Andrew Mawson and Partners, and exhibited at the Chelsea Flower Show in 1935. This was modified by Seely and Paget, and still further revised in consultation with John Gilmour, Assistant Director of Kew Gardens. The scheme that was eventually adopted featured a progression of garden areas similar to contemporary gardens at Sissinghurst, Kent and Great Dixter, Sussex. The ideas probably came from Stephen and Ginie; the plan was probably

implemented by a firm of nurserymen assisted by the Courtaulds' gardener, James Blackman.

The Courtaulds kept most of the existing trees, but added ornamental plantations, shrubberies and specimen trees – some of which were gifts from members of the royal family. In addition they laid out new garden areas. They were keen horticulturalists. Stephen had a passion for orchids which he raised in the glasshouses, and Ginie for roses which she obtained from the celebrated Sam McGredy nurseries at Portadown, Northern Ireland. (A red rose was later created in their Zimbabwean home and called 'Virginia Courtauld'). The 1930s planting is a mixture of informality – in the rockery east of the moat – and formality – on the west in the rose garden with its sunken pond and series of enclosed 'rooms'. Much of the structure and some of the original planting of the Courtauld era still survive.

Turning Circle and Palace Remains

As you leave the service wing, on your right is the north stone bridge dating to the late fifteenth century. The stone coping (protective capping) is thought to have been salvaged from the crenellated parapet on the Great Hall which was removed in the nineteenth century. At the near end of the bridge are the remains of the brick inner gatehouse (see illustration, page 2).

The once enclosed medieval inner court (see plan, page 29) is now partially overlain by the Courtaulds' turning circle which contains a large lime tree planted by them. On this side the Great Hall is faced in Reigate ashlar, and the string-course beneath the twentieth-century parapet is decorated with grotesque heads. The grey brick building with red brick arches to the right was the squash court added by Seely and Paget. The Courtaulds also installed the Italian ornamental well-head. Around this was laid a lawn with scattered informal trees and stunning views across to London.

The turning circle and area around the squash court are rich in remains of the medieval palace. The lawn was partially excavated in the

Part of a scheme for the gardens drawn up by Seely and Paget, 1934. Some of the proposals were never carried out, such as a wooden Chinese bridge over the east arm of the moat

The sunken rose garden, with the squash court in the background, photographed before restoration. The diamond-pattern brickwork is part of Elizabeth I's new royal lodgings built in the 1580s

Floor tile from Bek's great hall dating from about 1300

1950s and 1970s to reveal remains of Bishop Bek's manor house – a great hall floored with tiles dating to about 1300 and a vaulted cellar, both of which have since been reburied. Exposed to view are the low-level remains of the west range of the later royal apartments, the king's to the south and the queen's to the west. The apartments included a gallery where the king could walk in the shade or out of the rain. At the far right, behind the well-head, are the exposed remains of an angular tower constructed of yellow brick, possibly part of Bek's work. The remains of Henry VIII's chapel, which were also exposed in the 1970s, have since been reburied.

St George by A Hardiman, 1930. The statue originally stood on the squash court in Carlos Place behind the Courtaulds' Grosvenor Square house

Squash Court

Go over to the squash court and follow the path that turns the corner and runs alongside the end of the court. In a brick niche is a bronze statue of *St George* by Alfred Hardiman, dated 1930. The shield is decorated with animals and birds representing countries of the British Empire.

In the Courtauld era the area between the squash court and the moat retaining wall contained a formal garden of oval beds, preserved from the garden of the nineteenth-century house on the site. In the middle was a sundial set on to a baluster (pillar) from Waterloo Bridge (demolished 1935–6). This garden was removed when the area was excavated in 1952 to expose the remains of seven arched buttresses inserted by Queen Isabella in 1315 to support Bishop Bek's moat wall.

Turn left and on your left is the conservatory attached to the squash court. This was used to display exotic plants grown in the glasshouses.

South Garden

A narrow arch beneath the holly hedge to the right leads to a sixteenth-century tunnel into the south moat. It originally led from the king's lodgings to Henry VIII's privy bridge, and thence to the garden. However, to appreciate the full extent of the gardens, cross the timber bridge over the moat.

The south lawn was occupied by the kitchen and several inner courtyards of the medieval palace, none of which has been excavated. Notable trees include *Catalpa bignonioides* (Indian bean tree), *Liriodendron tulipifera* (tulip tree), *Jugands regia* (walnut) and *Laurus nobilis* (bay). Rectangular beds at the top of the moat wall were planted with bedding tulips in spring and dahlias in summer.

At the foot of the moat wall, the long mixed herbaceous border was replanted in 2000 as part of the new south moat garden designed by Isabelle Van Groeningen.

Ginie outside the Drawing Room in about 1940 with her three dogs: Kaïs (the Afghan hound), Solfo (the poodle) – named after one of Stephen's brother Jack's racehorses, and Caesar (the Great Dane)

The bridge over the south moat. The oak bridge was designed by Seely and Paget but is supported by medieval brick and stone foundations which formed part of the main southern entrance to the palace

Beyond and to the left of the bridge lay a privy garden in the fifteenth century. This was greatly enhanced by Henry VIII who laid out hedges, arbours and a high wooden fence for privacy. There was a pleached (interlaced) alley of plum and cherry trees to shade archers shooting at the nearby butts. Beyond the privy garden, the palace was encircled by three parks used for hunting.

Sunken Rose Garden

To reach the sunken garden, turn right, pass a curved seat enclosed by clipped evergreens, and join the stone path which faces it. Created by Stephen and Ginie, the rectangular garden is enclosed by informal hedges and the moat wall. At the centre of the pool was a bronze fountain of a boy and fish bought by Stephen in Florence; this was a copy of Verrocchio's late fifteenth-century sculpture in the Palazzo Vecchio in the same city. (The fountain is a gift from the family and is currently awaiting conservation.) The pool is planted with water lilies and surrounded by four Irish yews, rose beds, and a low brick wall topped by a lavender hedge.

Garden Rooms

Continue beyond the sunken garden into two consecutive 'garden rooms' divided by shrubbery; these have borders on the outer edges containing winter and spring planting. They terminate in a formal pool of water at the end of the moat, with a fountain as focal point, partially enclosed by tree and shrub planting including multi-stemmed trees of *Ligustrum lucidum* from China and *Poncirus trifoliata* (a hardy citrus relative). To the left of the pool you can see the Chauffeur's Block, including the garage designed by Seely and Paget (see panel, page 24). To the right are the remains of four bay windows added by James I to the queen's apartments in 1603.

North Moat and East Garden

Continue on the far side of the moat, under the stone north bridge which was probably built by Edward IV in the 1470s. Within the moat wall beyond the bridge is a stone window moved here from elsewhere in the palace. The lion and unicorn supporters are an example of architectural salvage. They are from Charles

COURTAULD'S CARS

TOPHAM PICTURE LIBRARY

The Courtaulds' Burney Streamline with its grey and blue chassis being admired outside Burlington House, Piccadilly in 1932. Only twelve were ever produced, one of which was owned by The Prince of Wales

Stephen owned at least one Rolls Royce, but from before the First World War he particularly favoured Mercedes cars, one of which Ginie also owned in the 1930s. In 1931 he bought one of the revolutionary and sensational Dennis Burney Streamlines (Stephen and his brother Jack were both directors of the company). Among the features were hydraulic brakes, independent suspension and a rear engine, giving a smooth, quiet ride even at 80 miles per hour. The seven-seater car was expensive by 1931 standards, costing £1500 (about the price of a four-bedroomed detached house in Eltham at the time).

Herbert Moore, Stephen's batman during the First World War, went on to serve as his chauffeur until his retirement in 1947. There is a family story of 'Old' Moore driving through Europe to Istanbul to meet the Courtaulds in their yacht as prearranged. On arrival, Stephen told him there had been a change of plan, and Moore promptly commenced the long journey back to England.

ROYAL HORTICULTURAL SOCIETY

N.R.

The orchid Vanda lombokensis *'Virginia Courtauld', created by Stephen. It was awarded a first-class certificate by the Royal Horticultural Society in June 1942*

RIGHT *A brick bastion on fourteenth-century stone footings at the south-east corner of the moat*

summer, and the strawberry tree *Arbutus unedo*, an evergreen with lily-of-the-valley flowers and strawberry-shaped fruit in autumn. Nearer the car park was the former tiltyard of the palace. The timber-clad pavilion was adapted by Seely and Paget from Victorian stables to serve the Courtaulds' former hard and grass tennis courts.

At this point you can turn left and return to the car park via a pedestrian gate near the Courtaulds' brick quadrant rose garden.

In the 1930s the area now occupied by the car park comprised a large rectangular utility area, with glasshouses and sheds built for the Courtaulds. They included two orchid houses as well as a carnation house, peach house and vinery. Orchids were Stephen's particular passion and he received awards from the Royal Horticultural Society for their propagation.

Alternatively you can continue south, past a flowering tulip tree (*Liriodendron tulipifera*) in the moat bank. To the right there is another fine view of the Courtauld wing, while to the left is a hedged swimming pool (now filled in) and an octagonal timber changing room. (By 1935 a swimming pool was considered indispensable for a country house.) Follow the moat bank and continue to the south timber bridge again; from here take the sloping path to the right which leads down into the dry area of the moat. Cross the moat to the corner bastion, keeping the moat wall on your left.

Barry's Palace of Westminster and were obtained by Rab Butler (see page 40) during restoration work in 1935. Beyond the bridge, take a stepped path within the bank at the point where the moat turns a corner. Turn right at the top and you see a fine view of Seely and Paget's loggia and east wing, the latter featuring sculptures representing Domesticity by Carlton Attwood. The eastern ridge is lined with trees and shrub planting. Notable plants are *Cornus mas* (Cornelian cherry) bearing small yellow flowers in winter and small red berries in late

Rock Garden

In the eastern moat water was reintroduced in a serpentine shape, edged in concrete. The furthest bank was laid out as a rock garden constructed of weathered limestone blocks, planted with small Japanese trees, shrubs and herbaceous plants. This distinctive garden area is typical of the 1930s. A water feature comprises a series of pools and cascades descending to the moat. Ginie bought a pair of black-necked Patagonian swans which bred successfully in the moat. The idea of swans – which are royal birds – may have been inspired by a possible derivation of the place-name Eltham from the Anglo-Saxon word for 'swan' ('elfetu').

Go up the steps in a bastion made by Seely and Paget in 1935 which leads to the loggia and pergola.

Triangular Garden

To the right, an awkward narrow corner between the new building and the old walls is filled by a triangular garden. A brick lattice pattern separates formal blocks of herbaceous planting.

Loggia and Pergola

Turn back to the loggia which is embellished with four reliefs carved by Gilbert Ledward, depicting some of the interests of Stephen and Virginia Courtauld. Walk under the pergola, covered in wisteria in summer; the stone Ionic columns were salvaged from the Bank of England in the 1930s and are probably late eighteenth-century in date.

Turn right and follow the Courtauld south front which is set back from the face of the Great Hall so as not to interfere visually with the medieval masonry. The south front contains the principal rooms including the Drawing Room, while above is a sculpture of Apollo, god of the arts (with a lyre under his arm), by Carlton Attwood. Climbers and shrubs were trained tightly against the wall.

The buttressed south-facing elevation of the Great Hall, overlooking the former kitchen courtyard, is constructed of Kentish ragstone which was inferior to the Reigate ashlar of the more prominent north front. A fine *Magnolia grandiflora* sits between two of the buttresses.

Now retrace your steps, turning right beyond the orangery, past the squash court and turning circle, and return to the service wing, or exit the site via the medieval stone bridge.

ABOVE *Reliefs by Gilbert Ledward on the loggia representing Stephen and Ginie's interests: Gardening, Yachting, Games (including badminton and quoits) and Mountaineering*

LEFT *The Pergola*

*The south front of
Edward IV's Great Hall,
with the Seely and Paget
wing beyond*

On first sight Eltham Palace presents two seemingly
unrelated faces: the remains of a medieval palace and
the Courtauld building of the 1930s. A closer look at
Eltham's history reveals the strands that link the two
periods and that have made Eltham the unique place it
is today. Stephen Courtauld himself showed a strong
interest in the origins of the site and, from his
collection of antiquarian works and local knowledge,
he developed a considerable understanding of its royal
history.

*Bishop Odo, who owned the manor
of Eltham, is shown on the Bayeux
Tapestry at the right hand of
William the Conqueror*

The Growth of the Royal Palace

In the Domesday survey of 1086 the manor of Eltham
is recorded as being in the possession of Odo, Bishop
of Bayeux, the half-brother of William the Conqueror.
The estate subsequently changed hands several times
until 1295 when the manor was acquired by Anthony
Bek, Bishop of Durham, a secular bishop, soldier and
statesman. The extent of Bek's work is not fully
known, but he certainly constructed a defensive stone
wall around the moat with brick bastions, accessed by

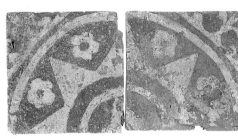

Floor tiles from Bek's great hall dating from about 1300. They are identical to tiles found at Lesnes Abbey near Erith, Kent, and were probably made by the same tilers

The spout of a jug, dating from about 1300, found in Bishop Bek's cellar during excavations in 1976

RIGHT *The coat of arms of Edward IV, builder of the Great Hall, in a stained-glass window by George Kruger Gray, 1936*

This gilded lead oak leaf formed part of the decoration on the choir stalls in Henry VIII's chapel

a timber drawbridge probably on the site of the present north bridge. He also created a park south of the moat which was later known variously as the Old, Middle or Little Park. Edward I and his son the Prince of Wales (the future Edward II) frequently stayed at Eltham, and in 1305 Bek 'presented' the manor to the prince, although he continued to live at Eltham until his death in 1311.

Edward II granted the manor to Isabella, his queen. Considerable improvements were made, including the construction of a new, stronger wall around most of the moat with buttresses at regular intervals. Edward and Isabella's second son John was born at Eltham in 1316 and was baptised in the chapel there. He was known as John of Eltham, a fact that might account for the palace erroneously being referred to from at least the early eighteenth century as King John's Court.

From the fourteenth century Eltham was one of the largest and most frequented royal residences in the country. Edward III spent much of his youth here and frequently visited it as king. There is a suggestion that the Order of the Garter – the oldest surviving order of chivalry in Europe – was established at Eltham in 1348 on Edward's return from fighting in France (at the start of the Hundred Years' War). The royal wardrobe accounts include twelve garters of blue embroidered with gold and silk with the order's motto 'Honi soit qui mal y pense' ('Let shame be to him who thinks this evil') which were supplied for a joust at Eltham. Such tournaments took place in the tiltyard which lay beyond the moat to the north-east. Extensive alterations and repairs were carried out in the 1350s and '60s, including the construction of new lodgings for the king and

queen on the east side of the island site. These featured a bathroom with a tiled floor and glazed windows for the king. South-east of the moat, further land was enclosed to create the Great Park for hunting; later, Richard II and his successors created the Lee, New or Horn Park to the south-west of the palace. Including Bek's 'Old' Park, the three parks comprised almost 1300 acres.

When the court was not in residence the palace would have been sparsely furnished. However, large sums continued to be spent on the buildings. Richard II created a herb garden on the south side of the palace beyond the moat in the 1380s 'for the King and Queen to have dinner there in the summer time', as well as a dancing chamber within the king's apartments. Henry IV spent ten of his thirteen Christmases as king at Eltham. He altered the planning of the palace in about 1400 by building a new set of timber-framed king's apartments on the west side. A corresponding set of lodgings was also built for the queen. Henry's chamber contained elaborate stained glass depicting his badge and motto 'Soveignez vous de moy' ('Remember me'). Henry VI became king at the age of nine months on the death of his father, and spent part of his boyhood at Eltham. In 1445 extensive additions were made to the queen's apartments for the arrival of his bride Margaret of Anjou.

Between 1475 and 1480 Edward IV constructed the Great Hall which still survives. When first built it had battlements on the sides and gables, and a lead roof. He built a new range of lodgings, and probably also the existing north bridge. During Christmas 1482 one of the most lavish feasts ever held in the palace was given for some 2000 people.

Notable Visitors to Eltham

Eltham continued to be frequented by the court until well into the sixteenth century, and during this time many international statesmen were entertained here. One of the most celebrated

Froissart presents his book to Richard II, from a fifteenth-century manuscript (the background is imaginary)

episodes took place in 1364 when Edward III received John II of France amid 'great dancing and caroling', when the latter returned to voluntary exile in England following his defeat in 1356 at the Battle of Poitiers (the most decisive English victory of the Hundred Years' War). John was accompanied by Jean Froissart, who subsequently recorded the event in his lively *Chronicles*. Froissart returned to Eltham in 1395 to present Richard II with a collection of his poems. In 1385 Leo V, the exiled King of Armenia, came to Richard's court at Eltham to solicit support in regaining his throne from the Turks. Five years later Richard's clerk of works, the poet Chaucer, was mugged twice on his way to the palace and lost £40 of official funds as well as his horse. Henry IV entertained Manuel Palaeologus, the Byzantine Emperor, at Eltham at Christmas 1400. In 1416 Sigismund, Holy Roman Emperor, discussed church affairs here with Henry V and forged an alliance with him. One of the most charming accounts concerns Prince Henry (later Henry VIII), much of whose boyhood was spent at Eltham. Here, in 1499, the nine-year-old prince met the Dutch philosopher Erasmus whom he challenged to write a poem. Within three days Erasmus duly produced a verse in praise of England, Henry VII, and the princes Arthur and Henry.

THE PALACE AT ITS PEAK

Two ground-floor surveys of Eltham Palace by John Thorpe of about 1603 depict the palace complex at its fullest development. The area occupied by the palace at its widest point was some 1000ft (305m) by 500ft (152m), which far exceeded that of Hampton Court.

The plan below depicts the moated site with angular corner turrets constructed by Bishop Bek enclosed by later buildings. Around the Great Court were timber lean-to galleries which gave covered access to the main residences: courtiers' lodgings on the east (left), and the queen's apartments on the west (right, with a series of bay windows built by James I in 1603–4). The king's apartments were in the top right-hand corner adjoining a small bridge which led into the privy garden. The range projecting into the Great Court is Henry VIII's chapel; above it is Edward IV's Great Hall with the royal apartments to the right. Above the hall is a series of smaller service courts including the Great Kitchens.

Thorpe also surveyed the Green or Outer Court beyond the bottom of this plan. This occupied the area now known as Courtyard, and included the timber-framed Chancellor's Lodgings as well as a range of service buildings supplying the palace's several kitchens and bakehouses.

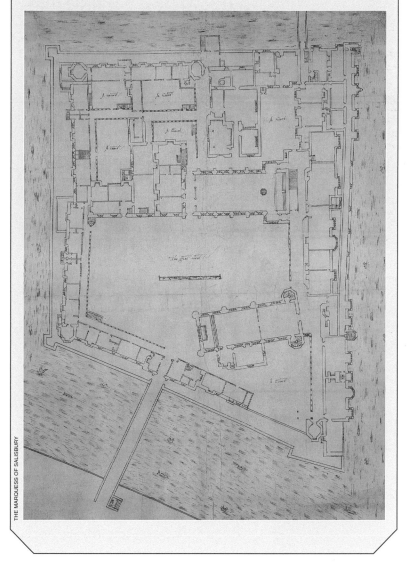

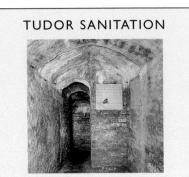

to reduce waste and control access to the king. The fact that they carry the name of Eltham is an indication of the palace's continuing importance at this period. Eltham was one of only six palaces large enough to accommodate and feed the entire court of 800 or more people. Henry VIII was, however, the last monarch to spend substantial amounts of time at Eltham, since Greenwich was more convenient and the hunting in Eltham's three parks was easily accessible from there.

TUDOR SANITATION

Part of the Tudor drainage system with a panel celebrating the investigation of the tunnel in 1834

A regular water supply was needed to allow for food preparation and sanitation for large numbers of people at the palace. This was initially supplied by wells, but in 1482 a brick conduit – which still survives – was built some two-thirds of a mile (1km) to the east of the palace. Water was carried in lead or hollow yew pipes to the kitchens, lodgings (including the bath house) and laundry.

An intricate network of underground tunnels at Eltham has given rise to rumours of secret passages leading to Greenwich Palace and underground stables. In fact it was part of Henry VIII's drainage system which conveyed liquid waste from the kitchens. Other brick tunnels were connected with the garderobes (lavatories), which were regularly flushed with clean water, while pits collected solid matter which was periodically shovelled out by highly paid royal servants known as 'gong fermers'.

The sixteenth-century range in The Courtyard was occupied in the 1580s by Sir Christopher Hatton, Elizabeth I's Lord Chancellor

The philosopher Erasmus, one of Eltham's illustrious visitors, in a portrait by Holbein

Henry VII and Henry VIII

Henry VII 'set up the faire front over the moat' according to a 1570s account; this probably refers to the west front which housed the royal apartments (now destroyed). In the 1520s extensive works were in progress for Henry VIII, including new king's lodgings, alterations to the queen's lodgings and the construction of a new chapel of Reigate stone. The chapel was as large as the Great Hall and stood within what is now the turning circle. The density of building within the walls of the moat left little space for gardens, and a new privy garden was constructed to the south and east. This included alleys and arbours, a bowling green and archery butts.

In 1525 the 'Eltham Ordinances' were drawn up here by Cardinal Wolsey. These were the regulations of the royal household, which aimed

Elizabeth and the Early Stuarts

Queen Elizabeth visited Eltham only occasionally although initially the palace was kept in good repair, and a new west front to the sovereign's apartments was built in the 1580s. In 1603, however, James I found it 'farre in decay' and in 1604 substantial repairs were undertaken and some alterations made to the queen's apartments. By this stage much of the palace was apparently given over to a variety of tenants connected to the court. In 1609 a German scientist Cornelius Drebbel was given rooms in which to set up his inventions; these included an astronomical clock known as the 'Eltham motion', which displayed the time, the hours of sunrise and sunset, the signs of the zodiac, the distance between the sun, moon and earth, the phases of the moon and the height of the tide.

Charles I was the last king to visit the palace.

Rich the Rebel

During the seventeenth century the palace buildings again fell into decay; in 1617–18 and again in 1631–32 there are reports of parts of the palace collapsing. In 1648 Parliamentary troops were quartered at Eltham to quench a revolt in Kent, and much of the palace and the royal parks were ransacked. Following the Civil War a Parliamentary survey of 1649 concluded that Eltham was 'much out of repair, and soe not tenantable', and all the good timber within the parks was felled for the use of the Navy. The manor was sold to Colonel Nathaniel Rich who demolished substantial parts of the site. When the diarist John Evelyn visited Eltham in 1656 he lamented that 'both the palace and chapel [are] in miserable ruins, the noble wood and park destroyed by Rich the Rebel'.

Restoration to the Crown

At the Restoration of the Monarchy in 1660 the palace reverted to the Crown, but the remaining buildings (notably the hall and chapel) were in ruins. Sir John Shaw leased the manor in 1663, but he never lived at the palace. Instead he employed the architect Hugh May to build Eltham Lodge in the former Great Park (now the Royal Blackheath Golf Club House).

The scientist Cornelius Drebbel. The clock Drebbel worked on at Eltham is referred to in Ben Jonson's play The Silent Women

The west front of the palace engraved by Peter Stent in about 1653. The tall ranges to the left and right are the queen's apartments (built about 1604) and the king's apartments (1580s); both enjoyed fine views towards London

Eighteenth-Century Antiquarian Interest and the Hall under Threat

During the eighteenth century various tenants put the palace remains to agricultural use. The Great Hall became a barn, the window tracery gradually decayed and many of the windows were partially bricked up. The palace site deteriorated into a picturesque ruin, attracting artists and antiquarians who clambered over the stonework and explored the tunnels. In 1782 a paper on Eltham was published in *Archaeologia*, accompanied by three prints by the artist Samuel Grimm. This fuelled further interest in the site, and artists such as Paul Sandby,

Thomas Girtin and J M W Turner depicted it more than once.

The remains were also the subject of architectural enquiry: for example, drawings of architectural details were published by H Dunnage and C Laver in *Plans and Elevations ... of the Great Hall of ... Eltham* (1828).

At this time interest in Eltham reached a peak, as a result of a threat to the Great Hall. In 1827 George IV's architect Jeffry Wyatville announced his intention of dismantling the roof and re-erecting it as part of the new St George's Hall at Windsor Castle. This proposal was abandoned owing to the decayed state of the timbers, but later in the year a gale damaged the roof and the Office of Woods and Forests advocated demolition. A vigorous preservation campaign was mounted, led by the Marquis of Lansdowne and Princess Sophia of Gloucester (who was Ranger of Greenwich Park). The campaign was successful and as a result the Great Hall, instead of being demolished, was propped and repaired under the supervision of Sir Robert Smirke.

The moated site had ceased to be a farm by the early nineteenth century. In 1818 a tenant named Richard Mills had converted the farmhouse south of the bridge into a villa known as the Moat House, and in 1859 the tenant of Court Farm, Richard Bloxam, turned the farm dwellings adjoining the Great Hall into a gentleman's residence, renamed Eltham Court. The Great Hall became an indoor tennis court which visitors were allowed to view on application. Flower gardens and kitchen gardens were laid out in the west and south parts of the moat.

RIGHT *The sole surviving medieval pendant from the Great Hall roof, published by J C Buckler in 1828. This provided the evidence for Seely and Paget's restoration of the pendants in 1934–35*

The east end of the Great Hall under repair in 1912. The timber frame of the medieval screens passage is infilled with nineteenth-century doors, windows and boarding

The Office of Works

In 1894–95 the Office of Works carried out minor repairs to the Great Hall, funded by the Society for the Protection of Ancient Buildings. More substantially, in 1903 the 'temporary' props inserted by Sir Robert Smirke were removed and the roof trussed up with steel beams bolted on to the timber. But the largest intervention to date occurred in 1911–14 when Charles Peers and Frank Baines, of the Ancient Monuments Division, systematically dismantled the Great Hall roof and reassembled it with the insertion of steel braces to strengthen the weakened timbers. The hall was re-roofed with tiles, and much of the tracery renewed in the bay windows. The north bridge was also repaired.

The ruined Great Hall and adjoining mid-nineteenth-century house known as Eltham Court, photographed in 1908

Watercolour by J M W Turner of the Great Hall being used as a barn, about 1790

The Controversial Courtauld Scheme

The late nineteenth and early twentieth centuries saw continuous suburban development of the area beyond the palace, and by the 1930s the site was almost surrounded by houses. In this context Stephen Courtauld's proposed scheme was welcomed as a means of halting the threat of creeping suburbanisation of the palace remains. There was nevertheless much debate about the propriety of building on to an ancient monument. Seely and Paget worked up a scheme in consultation with the landlord, the Commissioners for Crown Lands. They also discussed their proposals with Sir Charles Peers, by now President of the Society of Antiquaries and Chief Inspector of Ancient Monuments with the Office of Works, which was responsible for maintaining the Great Hall and ruins. Peers agreed with the general principle of the scheme on site in August 1933, on the eve of his retirement from the department. But he had not seen any of the plans, and when the Crown Lands duly approached the Ancient Monuments Board in September with plans and elevations, Sir Patrick Duff, the Permanent Secretary, was horrified. The conflict of interest was obvious: the Crown Lands wished to show a good return on their property, while the ideal solution for the Board would be to demolish the modern remains, grass over the site and trace the position of the former buildings within the turf. Duff wrote in protest to the Commissioner for Crown Lands in September 1933. Next it was suggested that the views of the newly established

SIR CHARLES PEERS
(1868–1952)

HULTON GETTY

Charles Reed Peers spent his early career in the office of the architect T G Jackson. In 1903 he became architectural editor of the *Victoria County Histories*. In 1910 he joined the Office of Works as an Inspector of Ancient Monuments, becoming Chief Inspector in 1913 until his retirement in 1933, the year in which he was awarded a Royal Institute of British Architects Gold Medal. His association with Seely and Paget continued after Eltham: as a governor of the Charterhouse in London he succeeded in appointing the firm to carry out the restoration and enlargement of the building after the war; he also worked with them on major repairs and new work at Eton College.

Crown Lands Advisory Committee be sought. The Committee's report concluded that the balance of argument was in favour of the Courtauld scheme. To pacify Duff, it was agreed that Seely and Paget would employ Peers as a consultant for the restoration of the Great Hall and north bridge. The Committee also insisted that the remains of the three fifteenth-century timber gables east of the Great Hall be preserved, a stipulation which profoundly influenced the eventual plan and design of the new building.

Seely and Paget's design for Eltham Hall, drawn by the young artist Lawrence Wright in 1934

John Seely and Paul Paget in the 1930s

Henry John Alexander Seely (1899–1963) was the eldest surviving son of the 1st Baron Mottistone. He read architecture at Trinity College, Cambridge where he met Paul Edward Paget (1901–85). In April 1926 the firm Seely and Paget was formed, with Paget running the administrative side of the office and establishing contacts with potential clients. They established themselves at Queen's Square Mews, where other residents included the architects Edwin Lutyens and Aston Webb, and Edward Hudson, founder of *Country Life*, a journal which enthusiastically reported some of Seely and Paget's early work. Their first domestic job was the restoration and alteration of Mottistone Manor on the Isle of Wight for Seely's father; minor domestic alterations for the actress Gladys Cooper and the playwright J B Priestley followed. By 1931 the firm had moved to 41 Cloth Fair, where it remained until 1986.

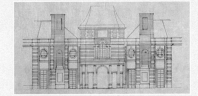

Seely and Paget's proposal for the loggia of their new wing at Eltham

In 1933 Eltham Palace represented Seely and Paget's most ambitious and challenging project to date. Other early work included church commissions such as St Faith, Lee-on-Solent, Hampshire (built 1933–34). The Second World War created opportunities for both secular and church restoration jobs, including repairs to a significant number of bomb-damaged London churches. The other major building type in which the firm specialised was educational – in the 1930s Seely and Paget designed chapels for Culham College, Oxford and Durham University.

Public Reaction

A leading article in *Architect and Building News* was headed 'Romance dies at Eltham' (though in truth much of the romance had gone with the large-scale rebuilding of the nineteenth century). The historian G M Young wrote in *The Times*: 'In order to provide the tenant with a modern mansion, three distinguished architects united their talents and intelligence to destroy one of the most beautiful things remaining in the neighbourhood of London … . The other day I found myself confronted with what at first I took to be an admirably designed but unfortunately sited cigarette factory.' The architect Herbert Baker was also critical; Gilbert Ledward countered, pointing out that at Soane's Bank of England building Baker had destroyed 'really beautiful work, while at Eltham everything of historic interest and beauty had been saved.'

The meeting of old and new: the glazed dome of the Entrance Hall is framed by the medieval timber gables and the west staircase pavilion, with the Great Hall beyond

The fifteenth-century gables being propped in 1933. The intention was to preserve them in situ, but during the building work this proved impossible and instead they were dismantled, restored and re-erected

1930s 'Mod-Cons'

Many of Eltham's technical features are taken for granted today, but in the 1930s they were by no means universal. By the mid-1930s the Central Electricity Board had created a national grid of high-voltage transmission lines which provided Britain with one of the most advanced systems of electricity supply in the world. The Courtaulds took full advantage of this and other new technologies to enhance their new home. There were electric fires and synchronous clocks in most rooms, and a loudspeaker system that could broadcast records throughout the ground floor. A private internal telephone exchange was installed by Siemens of London in 1936 (their main factory was in nearby Woolwich); even the bedrooms had internal telephones.

A centralised vacuum cleaner supplied by the British Vacuum Cleaner Company was located in the basement. The motor was connected by built-in pipes to sockets in the skirting of each room; a hose could be fixed to the sockets and dirt sucked down to the basement. The kitchen contained two Jackson's cookers and an electric Kelvinator refrigerator – cooking by electricity

An American advertisement for Kelvinator refrigerators, 1935; they were also manufactured in London

The motor of the centralised vacuum cleaner in the basement

was still relatively rare in the mid-1930s, and as late as 1939 only 2.6 per cent of the population owned a fridge.

Gas was used to run the central-heating system, which operated via coils embedded in the ceilings, except in the Entrance Hall, Great Hall and bathrooms where the heating was beneath the floor. This gave greater flexibility in room layouts as there were no radiators except in the bathrooms, which also contained heated towel rails for extra comfort and luxury.

THE *QUEEN MARY*

Detail of London buildings on the Queen Mary's *painted map*

Eltham's standard of services and design can be compared with Cunard Line's *Queen Mary* – 'the largest and most magnificent British liner that has ever been built' – which made her maiden voyage in May 1936. Elements of the *Queen Mary's* Art Deco interiors echo those at Eltham, such as the plaster reliefs and abstract carpets in the ship's main hall. As at Eltham, there was a considerable quantity of wood panelling (Cecil Beaton thought there was too much). A loudspeaker system broadcast music in selected areas. The cabin-class suites had panelled interiors, electric clocks, built-in furniture and telephones linked by an internal exchange. Most striking in comparison with Eltham was a large painted map of the North Atlantic by MacDonald Gill which hung in the cabin-class restaurant. In various shades of brown, the map featured contrasting elevations of famous buildings in London and New York. The similarities to the leather map in the Boudoir, and the Swedish and Italian scenes on the Entrance Hall panelling, are remarkable.

Stephen Courtauld's Art and Sculpture Collection

One of the specifications for the Courtaulds' new house was that it should provide a setting for Stephen's art collection. Stephen's elder brother Sam, chairman of Courtaulds since 1921, had established a fine collection of French Impressionist paintings at his home in Portman Square; this became the nucleus of the Courtauld Institute of Art (now housed in Somerset House). Stephen was more eclectic in his taste, and his art collection defies succinct classification.

Contemporary artists figure prominently, but Stephen avoided the avant garde and instead favoured artists trained in the classical tradition. He especially patronised artists connected with the British School at Rome, whose Honorary General Secretary, Sir Evelyn Shaw, was a close friend – in 1919 Stephen endowed a scholarship in engraving there and he served on its Council from 1921-47. Rome scholars whose work he purchased included the painters Winifred Knights and Tom Monnington and the sculptors and carvers Ledward, Jagger, Hardiman and H Wilson Parker.

The First World War made a lasting impression on Stephen, and he purchased a number of war-related works at an Imperial War Museum exhibition in 1919, including pieces by Frank Brangwyn, C R W Nevinson and Charles Pears. Paul Nash's celebrated watercolour *Hill 60* was purchased from the artist in 1920. Other artists whose work he collected included Muirhead Bone, Algernon Newton and Keith Baynes (the only artist who appears to have stayed regularly at Eltham). One of the few

paintings specifically commissioned by Stephen was L Campbell Taylor's portrait of himself and Ginie at 47 Grosvenor Square (see page 3).

The collection also included the work of earlier artists, such as a watercolour of *Folkestone Bay*, attributed to J M W Turner, and Turner's oil painting *The River Brent*, which hung in the Dining Room. A further fourteen Turner watercolours were displayed in the Library. Added to these were numerous watercolours and oils by other well-known English topographical artists: David Cox, J R Cozens, John Crome, Peter De Wint, Thomas Girtin, J S Cotman, Paul Sandby and Richard Wilson. The Drawing Room provided the setting for Stephen's collection of Old Masters: two Veroneses, a Tintoretto, a Bellini, and perhaps the most significant painting of all – *Christ in Limbo* by Mantegna.

The collection of European sculpture falls into two categories: Italian sixteenth-century bronzes and contemporary works commissioned by Stephen. The latter are dominated by the work of Rome scholars and include *The Sentry* by Jagger (in the Library), and the full-size *St George* by Alfred Hardiman (outside the squash court). The applied sculpture – on the exterior of the building and the panelling in the Drawing Room – was the work of Carlton Attwood and Gilbert Ledward. Lovatelli's statuary bust of Virginia was carved in Rome in 1923.

Frost Fair on the Thames in 1684 *by Jan Wyck. This was purchased by Stephen in 1926*

LEFT Place d'Armes, La Rochelle *by Keith Baynes, 1930. The painting depicts the Huguenot Courtaulds' ancestral homeland in north-west France. Both the Baynes and the Jan Wyck hung in the boudoir at Eltham*

Gilbert Ledward and Charles Sargeant Jagger as students at the Royal College of Art, 1912

The Arctic explorer Gino Watkins (centre) with Paul and Peter Peirano, taken shortly before Watkins's fatal second expedition to Greenland in 1932. Stephen had sponsored Watkins's first British Arctic Air-Route Expedition in 1930–31

Life at Eltham

The Courtaulds moved to Eltham on 25 March 1936. They soon established a daily routine comprising breakfast at 9am, lunch at 1pm and tea at 4.30pm; dinner was at 8pm. Among the notable guests was Queen Mary who visited twice. The late Queen Mother paid a private visit as Duchess of York in 1936 and regularly exchanged Christmas cards with the Courtaulds.

A selection of Stephen and Ginie's guests provides an insight into their broad social circle. They included: Freddie, the racing-driver Duke of Richmond; Terry, Lord Bective (whose firm provided the electrical installation at Eltham); the Conservative MPs Rab Butler and Leopold Amery (a fellow mountaineer and one-time president of the Alpine Club); Sir Ronald Storrs, former governor of Jerusalem and intimate of Lawrence of Arabia; Sir Stephen Gaselee, Librarian and Keeper of Records at the Foreign Office; Seely and Paget; Christopher Hussey, who wrote a series of articles on Eltham for *Country Life*; Evelyn Shaw of the British School at Rome; Sir Kenneth Clark, Chairman of the National Gallery;' the artist Keith Baynes; John Gilmour, Assistant Director of Kew Gardens; and Sir George Binney, an Arctic explorer in the early 1920s.

Full use was made of the grounds, which were opened to the public once a year. In the summer Ginie hosted 'at homes' commencing at 10pm and featuring fireworks and dancing well into the night. Annual 'Grand Summer Fêtes and Garden Parties' were also held. In 1938 the speeches were given by Sir Kingsley Wood,

Secretary of State for Air, followed by Sir Donald Somervell, the Attorney General. Side shows and 'refreshments at moderate prices' were available throughout the day, and a Grand Variety Concert was given by Fred E Wilton and his Whimsical Entertainers. The Courtaulds also hosted large dinners: for Peter Peirano's twenty-first birthday celebration in July 1937 the royal confectioners Gunter & Co supplied supper for 450 guests at 10 shillings per head excluding drink, while entertainment was provided by Lew Stone's celebrated dance band.

Eltham was something of a show house and was self-consciously luxurious. In winter the rooms were if anything regarded as too hot, as the heating could not be zoned. All the baths could be run at the same time if necessary so that guests could dress for dinner in comfort. Cecil Beaton neatly captured the decadence of the typical English country house party in 1933: 'The clock strikes, and there is a cocktail to impregnate one with energy enough to move from the depth of the sofa, to climb the stairs, and then there is the extravagance of soaking in a bath cloudy with salts'. Ginie was fastidious about food, and would ruthlessly make notes for the benefit of the cook during each course. Dinners at Eltham were not always a success, however, as Stephen and Ginie indiscriminately mixed people who may have had little in common. Furthermore if Stephen was in one of his introspective moods it was not unknown for him to sit through an entire meal without saying a word.

RIGHT *Stephen Gaselee (left, in characteristic spats, red socks and Old Etonian bow tie) with Stephen outside the Dining Room in about 1940. Gaselee was described at the time as 'the most erudite man in the world'*

Both Stephen and Ginie were keen on sport and Eltham could cater for energetic weekends. Ginie was an ardent squash-player and the court was always available, while in summer there was further opportunity for activity in the swimming pool and on the tennis courts. Table tennis and billiards were also provided, as well as chess for the less active.

Stephen and Ginie (above), and Mah-Jongg in his own deck chair (below), both taken on board the Virginia *in about 1935*

The Courtaulds spent long periods abroad and at such times the house was closed. Their first Christmas after moving into Eltham was spent in Cairo as part of an African tour which lasted from December 1936 to April 1937, while in 1937–38 they flew to Ceylon where they joined the *Virginia* to cruise around the South China Sea. Here they collected orchids and stored them on deck for propagation at Eltham.

EALING STUDIOS

Michael Balcon (1896–1977)

Stephen's main business interest in the 1930s was the development of Ealing Studios. He joined the board in 1931 and over the next twenty years made a significant personal and financial contribution towards the company's success. Throughout the 1930s the staple Ealing films were comedies starring Gracie Fields and George Formby. In 1938 Michael Balcon took charge of the production programme and oversaw the studios' golden age, developing a distinctive brand of film portraying British life in a wide variety of genres. During the war he made propaganda films that were both morale-building and didactic: *Next of Kin* (1942) carried the message 'Careless talk costs lives'.

The immediate post-war years produced a wide variety of films, including the epic *Scott of the Antarctic* with a score by Vaughan Williams. Ealing is now best remembered for the comedies which did much to boost public morale in the depressed social conditions of the late 1940s. The most outstanding year was 1949, when three 'classic' comedies were released: *Passport to Pimlico, Kind Hearts and Coronets* (with Alec Guinness as all nine members of the d'Ascoyne family) and *Whisky Galore* – a title rejected by the American censors and therefore released in America, at Stephen's wry suggestion, as *Tight Little Island*.

John Mills as Scott (left) and James Robertson Justice as Evans in Scott of the Antarctic *(1948)*

The Great Hall was regularly opened to the public and in 1937 Stephen published his own account of the palace which was sold for the benefit of the Woolwich Memorial Hospital

Wartime Eltham

The routine of daily life at Eltham was irreversibly interrupted by the war. An inventory was made of the entire contents of the house in December 1939, and the principal paintings, antique carpets and tapestries were dispersed for safe-keeping. The complement of domestic staff was difficult to maintain, and by the end of the war the pre-war army of about fifteen gardeners had been reduced to two.

The Courtaulds nevertheless remained at Eltham for much of the war, retreating to the basement during air raids. Both Stephen and Ginie contributed locally to the war effort, Ginie through the Women's Voluntary Service and Stephen with the Civil Defence. In September 1940, at the height of the Battle of Britain, over 100 incendiary bombs fell on the estate, four of them striking the Great Hall. The damaged roof was made good with a temporary covering but in April 1941 this was blown off when a parachute mine exploded to the south of the estate.

Courtauld hospitality continued throughout the war, but on a much reduced scale. From 1940, when he was bombed out of his London home, a room was reserved at Eltham for the Conservative minister Rab Butler, who was married to Stephen's niece. In July 1943 a party was held to mark the fifth anniversary of the Women's Voluntary Service, attended by 1000 guests.

In May 1944 the Courtaulds moved out of Eltham Palace. London society had changed irrevocably, and the lack of servants meant it

Family group on the lawn in 1940. LEFT TO RIGHT: *The photographer Iliffe Cozens, Stephen, Mollie and her husband August Courtauld (Stephen's cousin), Ginie and George Courtauld. Cozens and August Courtauld were both members of the British Arctic Air-Route Expedition, 1930–31*

> ### RICHARD AUSTEN BUTLER
> ### (1902–82)
>
>
>
> *Rab Butler photographed in 1941*
>
> Rab Butler was a relative by marriage of Stephen Courtauld and a close personal friend. He was Conservative MP for Saffron Walden and a junior minister in the Foreign Office in the early years of the war. In 1943, as President of the Board of Education, Butler worked on his white paper *Educational Reconstruction* while staying at Eltham where he discussed the draft with the Prime Minister Winston Churchill. The white paper formed the basis of his reforming 1944 Education Act which improved educational standards. Stephen's reaction to the white paper was favourable, although he regretted that provision had not been made for all secondary education to take place in boarding schools as he considered such 'disciplined corporate communities' would create an 'incalculably great' improvement in society.
>
> Butler's post-war offices were Chancellor of the Exchequer (1951–55), Home Secretary (1957–62) and Foreign Secretary (1963–64).

was impractical to continue living in the large house. The local bombing had greatly upset Ginie, and the couple had also had to endure the death on active service of their nephew Paul Peirano.

The lease for Eltham had a further eighty-eight years to run; the Courtaulds were willing to surrender this providing a suitable public use could be found for the property. Stephen was keen to find an educational use and following several months of discussion it was eventually agreed, in March 1945, to give the property over to the Army Educational Corps. Stephen presented his antique furniture, which was to remain in the Great Hall, on condition that he be consulted over any future proposals to build in the grounds.

Stephen and Ginie at Muckairn, Scotland, in about 1946

The Courtaulds after Eltham

In September 1944 Stephen and Ginie settled in Scotland on the 24,000-acre estate of Muckairn on the shores of Loch Etive in Argyll. Here Stephen was able to enjoy energetic walks, sketching and breeding pedigree Highland cattle. However, Ginie was restless and found the cold, wet winters uncomfortable.

In 1951 the couple moved to Southern Rhodesia (now Zimbabwe) and bought a parcel of land in the Imbeza Valley, Umtali (now Mutare). They built a new house, which they named La Rochelle after the home of Stephen's Huguenot ancestors in western France, and moved into it in September 1953.

In spite of increasing ill-health, Stephen continued to participate vigorously in projects concerning local social welfare and cultural life. At Mutare he built the Courtauld Theatre, the Queen's Hall in the Civic Centre, and a multi-racial residential club. In Salisbury (now Harare) he built a concert hall and helped fund University College, Salisbury. He was also instrumental in establishing the Rhodes National Gallery in Salisbury (now the National Gallery of Zimbabwe), and acted as chairman of the board of trustees from 1953 to 1961. He loaned and eventually bequeathed many of his works of art in order to help establish a national collection in the gallery. He also spent much time writing, and produced three volumes of *The Huguenot Family of Courtauld*, published between 1957 and 1967. He was knighted in 1958.

Stephen died in 1967 and Ginie stayed on at La Rochelle until 1970 when the guerrilla war in Rhodesia prompted her to move to Jersey where she remained until her death in 1972. La Rochelle is now an hotel.

Though less grand, the interior of the house at La Rochelle bears many similarities to Eltham. Around it the Courtaulds created an extensive botanic garden and arboretum

Stephen sketching at Loch Etive, Scotland, in about 1946

An Army officers' conference at Eltham in the late 1960s

ABOVE AND RIGHT: *The Great Hall roof being repaired by staff of the Ministry of Works in 1952*

The Army at Eltham

From 1945 to 1992 Eltham was home to a number of different units concerned with army education. Between 1945 and 1948 it was occupied by the Officers' Training Wing of the Army School of Education. The School ran courses in teaching method for officers returning home after service overseas, and for new entrants to the service. *The General Education Handbook* – a full guide for instructors - was produced at Eltham.

In October 1945 it was announced that Eltham would also become the home of the Army Educational Corps (the following year the corps received the 'Royal' prefix). Among the distinguished officers involved was Col Archie C T White, who had been awarded the VC in 1916 for action on the Somme. He served with the RAEC from 1920 until his retirement in 1947, and in 1963 wrote *The Story of Army Education 1643-1963*.

In 1948 the Institute of Army Education (IAE) – an executive and research establishment of the Directorate of Army Education under the War Office – came to Eltham. As well as providing the venue for educational conferences, the Institute also administered educational examinations for the Army, teacher recruitment for Army children's schools overseas and further education for regular soldiers and officers.

In 1983 another educational unit, HQ Director of Army Education, replaced the IAE. This and the Royal Army Educational Corps remained at Eltham until 1992.

The Ministry of Works

While the Army occupied the 1930s building, the Ministry of Works took over the maintenance of the Great Hall, the stone moat bridge and palace walls. The hall was opened to the public three days a week, with the emphasis on the medieval remains and an attempt to downplay the 1930s intervention. Unfortunately this included the removal of the ten gondola-style Courtauld lanterns. The floor was the subject of considerable debate between the Ministry's Inspector and the Army. The Inspector wanted a stone floor but the Army required a sprung floor for dancing. Eventually a compromise was reached: a stone floor was laid, but the Army was permitted to install a timber floor on top (now removed).

The Royal Parks maintained the gardens and used the grounds as a training establishment for apprentice gardeners between 1975 and 1993.

English Heritage Restoration

In 1984 English Heritage assumed responsibility for the Great Hall and in 1995 it took over the management of the entire site. The house and its 1930s interiors had remained largely intact, and English Heritage had two aims: to open to the public both the 1930s house and the palace remains and gardens; and to create a venue for conferences and other commercial events. In presenting the Courtauld wing, it was possible to build up a detailed picture of the original appearance of the rooms using the inventory compiled for the Courtaulds in 1939, the photographs taken for *Country Life* in 1936, and over 600 plans drawn by Seely and Paget. This documentary material, plus the results of historic paint analysis, assisted English Heritage in recreating the appearance of the wall and floor surfaces in the main rooms, partly funded by a generous grant from the Heritage Lottery Fund.

The Dining Room doors undergoing restoration by specialist conservators Schlapobersky & Boux

It would be impossible to reinstate fully the Courtaulds' collection of furniture and art – much of which has been dispersed as far as Zimbabwe. Instead, replica furniture has been installed in the Entrance Hall and Dining Room. In the Dining Room the bird's-eye maple flexwood veneer was reinstated, together with the dining furniture and carpet. The circular Marion Dorn carpet in the Entrance Hall was reproduced from the original in the Victoria and Albert Museum using the same technique as that employed in the 1930s. In the Great Hall the ten Courtauld lanterns were recreated, and

the timber decking removed to reveal the 1950s stone flagged floor which is close in spirit to the Courtauld floor. Elsewhere, the rooms contain a selection of period furniture and antiques representative of the Courtaulds' taste. The curtains and soft furnishings had also disappeared, but reproductions have been made using suitable textiles.

Many of Stephen Courtauld's paintings are now in private hands. Where possible these have been reproduced, since the Courtaulds' choice of paintings was important to the whole scheme of the room. Assistance with reproduction was generously given by the National Gallery, London. We are grateful to owners of works of art which once hung in the house for allowing us to reproduce them for display. Where reproduction was impossible, paintings from English Heritage's reserve collections have been hung.

The gardens are also being restored to their 1930s appearance.

The overall intention behind the restoration of Eltham Palace is to hint at the opulence of the Courtaulds' way of life here, set against the backdrop of one of the most important, but recently neglected, royal palaces of medieval England.

Recreation of the Marion Dorn carpet by Donegal Carpets in Ireland

The pink leather Dining Room chairs were copied exactly from photographs by cabinetmakers N E J Stevenson

Detail from the leather map in the Boudoir

ACKNOWLEDGMENTS

The author gratefully acknowledges the generous assistance of family members and friends of Stephen and Ginie Courtauld, as well as numerous colleagues who have commented on the text. Alan Powers and John Priestley have also kindly commented and the English Heritage Photography Department has produced outstanding images notwithstanding impossible deadlines.

FURTHER READING

The Royal Palace

R Brook, *The Story of Eltham Palace* (Harrap & Co, London, 1960).

H M Colvin (ed), *The History of the King's Works* vols II & IV (HMSO, London, 1963 and 1982).

C Hussey, 'Eltham Hall', *Country Life* (15, 22 and 29 May 1937), pp534–39, 568–73 and 594–99.

E J Priestley, *Eltham Palace* (forthcoming).

D E Strong, *Eltham Palace* (DoE Official Handbook, HMSO, London, 1983).

S Thurley, *The Royal Palaces of Tudor England* (Yale University, New Haven and London, 1993).

H Woods, 'Excavations at Eltham Palace, 1975–9', *Transactions of the London and Middlesex Archaeological Society* 33 (1982), pp215–65.

The 1930s

C Aslet, *The Last Country Houses* (Yale University, New Haven and London, 1982).

C Aslet, 'An interview with the late Paul Paget 1901–1985', *Thirties Society Journal* 6 (1987) pp16–25.

C Boydell, *The Architect of Floors: Modernism, Art and Marion Dorn Designs* (Schoeser, London, 1996).

P Skipwith, *Gilbert Ledward: A Centenary Tribute* (Fine Art Society, London, 1988).

J Steele, *Queen Mary* (Phaidon, London, 1995).

Thirties (Arts Council, London, 1979).

Stephen Courtauld

S L Courtauld, *Eltham Palace* (privately published, London, 1937).

S L Courtauld, 'The first ascent of the Innominata Face of Mont Blanc, 1919', *The Alpine Journal* LVII (1949), pp127–45.

S L Courtauld, *The Huguenot Family of Courtauld*, 3 vols (Curwen Press, London, 1957-67).

Published by English Heritage
1 Waterhouse Square, 138-142 Holborn
London EC1N 2ST

Copyright © English Heritage 1999

First published by English Heritage 1999
Reprinted 1999, 2000, 2004, 2006, 2008
ISBN 978 1 85074 734 5

Edited by Kate Jeffrey
Designed by Joanna Griffiths
Printed in England by the colourhouse
C110   10/08   06729

Unless otherwise stated all photographs were taken for English Heritage, whose copyright they remain.